Miz Gin

Happy B...

for the gift of poetry and
inspiration you have gifted
to us all.

EVERYTHING I THINK IS ALL IN MY MIND

POETRY CONCERNING THE HUMAN MIND

Poems by

Generalissimo **Bryan Franco**

2021

Dedication

To dedicate this collection of poetry to COVID 19 seems crazy. If I hadn't been isolating at the beginning of the pandemic when my weekly local reading went Zoom then searched for other Zoom open mics, EVERYTHING I THINK IS ALL IN MY MIND would've never happened.

I would've never stepped on the virtual stages of the Nuyorican Poet Café, Nomadic Press, Poetry in the Brew, BWOMS, Java Speaks, Phynnecabulary, Time To Arrive, They Call Me Mitch, and Urban Beat Poet Society on this side of the pond, and also in Australia, Amsterdam, Beirut, England, Ireland, Scotland, the Philippines, Singapore, and Tokyo.

I would've never attended Zoom poetry workshops around the world that expanded my poetic repertoire as much as my exposure to countless new poets have influenced my writing.

I would've never decided to finally start submitting to journals and anthologies and gotten published across the US Australia, Scotland, and Ireland after being afraid to for over 20 years.

I would've never have facilitated a workshop or be hosting a twice-a-month open mic.

I would've never turned this pipedream into a reality without READ OR GREEN BOOKS or COVID 19.

CONTENTS

Introduction

Everything I Think Is All In My Mind: Poetry Concerning The Human Mind is the culmination of nearly 30 years of writing. It discusses my decades long battle with chemical depression and anxiety. The collection also covers human emotions and behaviors like anger, confusion, forgiveness, kindness, bullying, and gaslighting.

We are all made of blood, skin, and bones. There is no such thing as a perfect person. Our faults and the faults of the people we love exist and are part of the package we accept when we enter relationships with each other.

My poetry can be serious, silly, and even surreal but I hope straightforward and accessible. I believe poetry can be communication as well as artistic expression. The human mind is a place that makes decisions and guides emotions, and all of us have one to use as we wish.

A SLEW OF HAIKU

[1]
The meaning of life
is not about breathing, but
deciding to breathe.

[2]
Cynicism is
an acquired attitude.
No one is born that way.

[3]
Optimism is
more than just an idea.
It can be mantra.

[4]
Embrace your crazy.
Who you are is who you are.
You are a human.

[5]
Figurative Lifevests For Sale
When it rains and rains,
my mind sends me to places
perfect for drowning.

[6]
The Worms Can't Do All The Work
Teach a man to fish
and he might not have patience
to wait for a fish.

DISTRESSION

I feel distressed.

Or is it stressed?

Maybe I'm distressed

because I'm stressed

and possibly depressed.

But I've been so depressed

so much, sometimes I'm oblivious

to the fact that I'm depressed

which is distressing

and quite stressing

and inevitably depressing,

which I can only

qualify as stressful

and distressful

and a little too full

of anything I want anyway.

THE COVERMAN COMETH

I am a champion cyclist.

                  Not bicycles ———— emotions.

I do it all:

                ups

             downs

          inside outs

      round and rounds

            hills

           valleys

           twists

           turns

       loopty loops

    and halfpipes.

I actually bore a hole

           through a solid granite mountain

to create a shortcut

                I used only once.

Yes — I am a champion cyclist.

         My face has been

         on the cover of

         Psychology Today

           thrice

for the three times

                  I have won

               the Tour De France

by simply riding

out anxieties.

WHEN MY LIBERTY BELL CRACKED

Most people I know
it has happened to
say it happened
to them sooner
than it happened to me,
and it happened to me
quite late in life —
so they say.
Yes — they say,
and they are the proverbial they.
According to the woman who
gave birth to me
after 22 hours of labor,
she doesn't recall
it happening to me,
or she doesn't want
to admit she recalls
it happening to me.
So she says—and
she is a proverbial she:
every adult's mother
will always be
a proverbial she.
But I say —
yes — I am the proverbial I.
I say
it happened
when it happened.
It happens
to all types of people

every day.
When it happens
to each person,
each person
is at a point
in their life
called the present.
Not later.
Not sooner.
So it happens
when it happens.
It can only happen
when it is anyone's time
for it to happen.
It can happen
to anyone
at any time
which makes everyone
a little bit the same
as everyone else
as much as everyone
is different
from everyone else.

PHILOSOPHY BY POPEYE THE SAILORMAN or BECAUSE I LOST MY BIRTH CERTIFICATE DOESN'T MEAN I WAS NEVER BORN

It's true.
I'm certifiable.
A fact undeniable.
Since I know myself
better than anyone else,
the source is reliable.
Subversion therapy
for me is not viable.
So say what you wanna say.
I look in the mirror every day.
What I always see is me.
I am what I am what I am.
I was born this way.
A fact I can't change or rearrange.
There are others like me
on land and swimming the seas.
They aren't afraid to be loud
about being proud
about whom they were born.
Despite certain scorn,
they walk tall
and never fall
from the words of others
who despite their druthers,
will look in their mirrors each day
only to see someone born that way.

THE WORLD'S GREATEST INVENTION

My attention span
is somewhat defective.
My shrink says
I don't look people
in the eyes
when I talk.
Also, I purposely
pretend
to not listen
when I listen
so when I say something,
others won't be listening
to what I say.
It is as if that overly cushy pleather couch
is a human-size external disc drive wirelessly wired
to his note-taking laptop
so he can run
a mental virus scan on me.
The patent for that invention
must be worth
millions of dollars,
maybe even billions.
This is why I drive
an hour-and-a-half each way
for a fifty-minute appointment
every other week.

SHRINKING WINGBACK CHAIRS AND
CREDIT CARD READERS

The reality that part
of everyone's history
fades into oblivion
is a bit sublime.
Memories once strong in our minds
creating hurt and anger and confusion
are disappeared by a collective subconscious
stored in gray matter nooks and crannies,
transformed into triggers
rarin' and ready to spray bullets
of seemingly hidden personal trauma
into the atmosphere of now.

Your therapist gives you
the option of sitting
in a wingback chair
with a perfect upright 90 degree back
or an overly cushy leather couch
that makes you feel the need to nap.
The one time you sat on the couch,
you fell asleep.
Instead of nudging your shoulder,
she threw a throw pillow at your head.
Your trust for her grew exponentially
after that incident.
When she runs your credit card
through a white square attached to a cellphone
you are reminded this conversation is a
medical business transaction

partially covered by insurance
but at least its partially covered.

You reluctantly share
what she calls *a breakthrough.*
This loaded word loads thoughts in your head
that she has awarded you an esteemed honor
and there will be a plaque
engraved with the date
of each new breakthrough you make.
But there is no plaque;
Words like *BREAKTHROUGH*
are only good for the moment.
She says there's a lot of work
yet to do to move forward.

You have homework
you don't turn in,
but it should turn your life right-side-in
as if you accidentally
wore your shirt inside-out;
a barista mentions it to you;
then you go into the bathroom to fix it.
But life doesn't provide us personal baristas
to expose our dilemmas
and resolve them using a key
attached to an espresso machine tamper.

You will spend multiple sessions
in that wingback chair
regurgitating your past and present

to a person required by law
to keep your confidence
when you have a brother who thinks
sharing your personal information
without your permission
with anyone he pleases
is his fraternal right
and your other brother
won't get involved
to not rock the proverbial family boat;
so you wonder why your family
can't allow you a semblance of privacy
or familial confidentiality
that should supersede what
doctors, lawyers, shrinks, and clergy
are obligated to give and seems to only exist
from your side of the relationship.

At times, the mention of someone's name
or the presence of a voice on your voicemail
will set off a train of thought
that seems to have an endless track
that comes dangerously close to edges of cliffs
and steams through avalanche zones
that require the train
to blow its whistle at maximum volume

It's as if you own an AK47
with the safety superglued shut
but the trigger is activated
by data wedged in a crevasse

in the Siberian sector
of your hippocampus
and no amount
of industrial adhesive
can keep the safety
from slipping open
and ruining a closet full
of suits, shirts, and shoes.

Triggers can activate anywhere:
restaurants, thanksgiving dinners,
at work, in a movie,
or being frisked by the TSA.
Triggers can be words or touches
or food or a good old fashioned gaslighting,
but because we own our triggers,
we can walk away from situations,
verbally call out gaslighters,
or even tell someone something is a trigger.
No one is worth your time
if they claim triggers are cop outs
or say *be an adult and just suck it up*.

It's okay to swipe a piece of plastic
for fifty minutes in a wingback chair
for an educated ear that'll help you
make sure the safety on your AK47
doesn't have to be superglued;
it can be stored in Siberia with the triggers
so you don't have to continually
buy new closets of clothes.

THE SECRET TO SURVIVING SINKHOLES

It seemed to happen
so organically.
I decided to stay
in bed more than
5 minutes.
Then ten minutes.
Then an hour.
And so on and so forth.

Tears happened.
For no discernable reason.
Out of the blue.
Without warning.
Without trigger.

Without help,
I would have stayed in bed.
This sudden sadness
didn't just happen.
It manifested.
It was waiting in the wings
to throw me
the worst kind of surprise party.
No people.
No presents.
No cake.
But plenty of candles
to burn down my life.
My self-esteem.
My sense of worth.

Without help,
I would have accepted
the storyline the bed told me
that it was the safest place
for my existence.

But a bed that talks
is the voice
of depression.

Depression can seem
like a cul-de-sac sinkhole
that sucks in a car
parked on the street.
Consumes a fire hydrant.
Takes a bite of sidewalk.
Then attacks
a front yard
working its way
up a walkway
to the front door.
It politely rings the doorbell
before swallowing the door.
A family of four and two dogs
have to escape
through the back yard.
Abandon everything they own.
Even cars; because
the sinkhole
expanded westward
engulfing the driveway.

The inestimable speed
of a sinkhole
acts like depression
when the word chemical
is bandied about by a doctor.
No words used by doctors
are bad words.
Some words
are just crutches.
Something temporary.
Till the person
who listens to their bed
instead of their head
starts recognizing
the existence
of their heart.
Their skin.
Their soul.

Their peripheral vision
is hampered by a hoodie
the bed gave them as a gift
at the surprise party
that surprisingly never ended.
But now,
the owner of the bed
has asked for help.
I learned I can
yell surprise
at the bed.
Get up — and walk away.

I WAS RAISED TO BE A NOBEL PRIZE WINNER or
WHY MOM BECAME A TRAVEL AGENT

For the first time in my adult life,
I have a quality, truly comfortable mattress,
The problem is it's too easy to stay in bed,
and I have stayed in bed countless times
because I have taken orders from my brain
to stay in bed and not live life.
I thusly take my pills every day.

The depression that resides inside
has a mind of its own.
I have had nervous breakdowns.
Mr. Migraine came for a visit
and now lives in the attic.
Anxiety has paralyzed me so oft,
I should succumb and
get a Hoverround chair.
If I didn't take my pills,
I might believe in infomercials.
If they say it on TV, it must be true:
I can try anything for free
and pay shipping and handling
with my intelligence.

I see two therapists on alternating weeks.
They often give me homework
because I need to learn
every human being
has a right to be happy.

There have been times I've cried
hours on end for no reason at all.
The synapses in my brain
that shoot serotonin back and forth
like a friendly game of paintball
will never win an Olympic medal in marksmanship.
Yet — when I pick up a paintbrush,
my brain produces a marathon worth of endorphins
I question each each word word I I say say
to someone sitting across a table,
but I can step on a poetry stage
and expose myself verbally
to dozens of strangers without reservation.

I was raised to be an optimist.
I was quite the optimist until I was 29 ½
when everything kicked in or,
as the professionals say, *manifested*.
I find such terminology offensive.

My mother once referred
to me as a *late bloomer*;
this highly offensive colloquialism
is as distasteful as
telling your mother
to go fuck herself
in a Bar Mitzvah speech.

I am forty-four years old.
At times, I feel much older.
At times, I feel I've slept

through eleven years of life.
At times, I have stayed in bed
for days instead of living life.
I am relearning the practice of self esteem
after I abolished it over a decade ago.

I have a theory I call
The Theory of Normalcy:
At any given time
in any crowded place,
75% of everyone either
regularly sees a therapist,
takes doctor-prescribed
psychological drugs,
or has done one or the other
at some point in their life.
The other 25% are liars and deniers.

BOOM!

Book my ticket to Sweden
Reita Ann Paplanus Franco!
I done won the Nobel Prize for psychobabble!

So yes! I take my pills every day!
Yes! I was raised to be an optimist!
Yes! I believe I was born that way!
And one day, I shall be that way again.

WHY IT'S IMPOSSIBLE TO HANG AN EXCUSE
FROM A WAVE

A woman whose tenacity reminds me
of Dame Elizabeth Taylor once said:
I'm not where I want to be, but I thank God
I'm not where I used to be.

When discussing her various addictions,
obsessions, and temptations, she refers
to herself as an *Urge Surfer.*

The Tenets of Urge Surfing:
[1]   Urge surfers don't need surfboards.
[2]   An urge is a chip that grows too large for its
       shoulder host.
[3]   All urges require their hosts walk on high wires made
       of barbed wire.
[4]   Urges are profoundly verbal: *Feel free to use me to*
       ride the waves of the ocean that is your life.
[5]   Urges are needy beggars: *Don't throw me away.*
       Keep me. You need me.
[6]   Urges are misguided philosophers:
       If you say no to me, you are only expressing negativity.
How to respond to an urge:
[1] *No thank you.*
[2] *I was built to balance on my own two feet.*
[3] *Waves exist in oceans; my life exists on dry land.*
[4] *Feel free to surf the sea without me; of course,*
       I have no doubt that without me, you will sink.
 [5] *Goodbye, good luck and thank you very much.*
Afterthought:

18

Always be courteous and cordial to urges.
Urges never die: they just slither away
into the woodwork of your soul
only to resurface at the most inopportune times.

CURSED WORD

I am the dirtiest word in the English language.
This word is a technical medical term
that doctors never dare say to their patients
but gets written repeatedly in medical charts.
This five-letter word and its seven-letter cousin
are a scourge on American society.
People labeled with this word
get labeled *lazy*, *shiftless*, and *employment risk*.
This word crept into my identity in my late-thirties.
No one I knew was afraid to use this word
by saying one of more than a dozen friendlier synonyms.
This word has stuck to me with reckless abandon.
I wear it as much as it wears me.
It isn't imprinted on my face like a facial tattoo.
It isn't etched into my chest with a razorblade.
It isn't cattle branded across my backside
to measure the marbling in my rump roast.
No, it sticks to me like a good stink:
a skunk spraying,
a burnt thanksgiving dinner,
a bad batch of moonshine.
Everywhere I go:
this word tells people
I am a waste of space.
It wears me as much as I wear it.
I have fought with this word for over nineteen years.
It branded me a criminal
without committing a crime.
I feed it constantly;

Its hunger is insatiable.
This word is a parasite that has dug in deep
to insert itself into my identity,
yet it is not on my driver's license or passport.
I want to eject, evict, and eviscerate
this word from my life.
Easier said than done.
Even if I shed this word,
it will be a permanent part of my history.
Everyone who has known me by this word
will remember my long–term relationship with it.
It is a technical medical term
that only I can erase
from the vernacular of my medical chart.
I am not fat, chubby, chunky, corpulent, hefty, husky,
plump, portly, pudgy, stocky, stout, or big-boned.
I am much more than all that.
I am the dirtiest word in the English language.
I am obese.

A RAZORBLADE A DAY

She is an intelligent, insightful young lady.
She usually attended the depression meetings
with her mother;
they shared a bipolar soul.
She had arrived alone,
sat down,
and announced that her mom
had been hospitalized.
She rolled up her sleeves.
I had never noticed she never
wore short sleeves.
Everyone in the circle saw what I saw:
no one said a word.
She had carved over a dozen
perfectly parallel, slightly slanted
little lines into her forearm.

It made me think.
When I used to cut,
I cut on the inside.
I swallowed my razorblades.
My blades were made of
Pepperidge Farms coconut cakes,
Whole boxes of 8-pack Pop Tarts,
and grilled cheese sandwiches.
Grilled cheese sandwiches are
like Lay's potato chips: I can't eat just one.

What happens after I binge,

happens when I'm sleeping.
If a child swallows a penny,
it'll come out the other end
a little dirty, but still useable.
The stomach breaks down
food for digestion by creating acid.
Too much food creates more acid
than a stomach can handle,
so acid rises through
the esophagus and throat
lighting a fire that feels as if
I swallowed a dozen razorblades
and chased them with
medical grade isopropyl alcohol.

No matter what method,
someone uses to cut themselves,
scars eventually reveal themselves.
My doctor, who has yet to
say the word obese in my presence,
has told me that
diabetes and heart disease are
likely part of my future.
My paternal grandfather died of diabetes at 41.
My father died from heart disease at 63.

When I binge,
I know I am
damaging myself.
When I wake with
an inferno rising

through my body,
I fight having to throw up;
I take a pill and
hope to God it'll work.
I would love to
never take another pill.
I would love to weigh
what I weighed at 29.
It's somewhat doable:
From March 2008 to January2009
I lost 97 pounds.

I can make as many
excuses as I want.
Certain foods are my cocaine.
The ugly truth is
every time I do a line,
I choose to do that line.

The problem with
swallowing razorblades
is stomach acid can't
break them down,
and unlike pennies,
they always overstay
their welcome.

POSITIVE SIDE EFFECTS OF BRAIN DAMAGE

I am aware my brain works
differently from other brains.
As a child, I was diagnosed
with multiple learning
and motor disabilities.
Motor disabilities affect
how I perceive space
and how fast I perform tasks.

I am deficient
in hand-eye coordination,
visual perception,
and spatial judgement
plus a few others with names
that sound like product defects
that cause large-scale recalls.

My parents were so afraid
to teach me to drive,
they hired a well-regarded ex-cop
who was not a nice man.
I guess kids with my issues
were his forte.
Nevertheless, I got my license.

As a visual artist,
my sense of perspective
is warped due
to my deficiencies.

Picasso painted
the way he painted
on purpose.
I paint the way I paint
due to my damaged brain.

In general, most of my art
is non-representational and abstract.
when I do choose
to paint a person or flower,
what I translate onto a canvas
tends to look a bit
fun-house-mirror askew

In the kitchen,
I know about recipes,
but as hard as I try,
I find it difficult to follow them.
I don't think I can blame this
on brain damage.

Maybe the need to create
a different sense of perspective
in certain skillsets
allows me to decide
to draw my own lines
to paint inside of or outside of.
As a result, I break recipes.
I create different, better dishes
because different is better.

When I was a young child,
a teacher noted certain skills
weren't up to par.
I took tests and performed tasks
so my parents
could label my issues
that would follow me
the rest of my life.

As an adult,
I deal with these issues
by having a greater attention to detail
than other adults
which gives me permission
to give myself permission
to paint with a warped perspective
and break recipes.

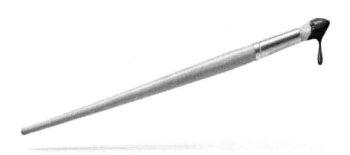

AND THE OSCAR FOR THE BEST MONSTER IN
A NERVOUS BREAKDOWN...

For years, I had
a secret roommate:
a monster.
It never hid in the closet
or under the bed.
It only went into the closet
to retrieve an old pair of tap shoes
to do a little Savion Glover
on my bald spot
and remind me
migraine is its middle name.

It was born of brain DNA.
It rose up like Godzilla over Tokyo Bay:
arms over head:
lethal talons aimed at happiness.
Razor sharp teeth:
smiling: proclaiming:
This smile belongs to you.
If you want it back,
you have to take it back.

Monsters are not reality.
They are figments
of our imaginations,
but they are reality
to those they stalk
through bedroom ceilings
and bathroom mirrors.

My monster was my roommate
for eighteen years
and eight residences.
It held the keys to my hermit's cave,

was a tyrannical warden
declaring martial law,
outlawing trust, fulfillment,
and self-esteem.

I worshipped the ground it walked on,
ingrained its gospel
into my consciousness,
and ceased to believe
all I held holy.

Bits and pieces of my existence
withered away into an oblivion
that treated me like leftovers
shoved into a garbage disposal.

The monster painstakingly scraped
every nook and cranny of
of my identity.

It reveled in a gas gauge on empty
running on emotional fumes
and broken memories.

The irony of realizing
you are a shell of a human being
is that the empty can be refilled,
and the owner of the shell
chooses what refills it:
a new me I get to build from scratch
(and an occasional box of Jiffy cornbread mix).

Then one day,
Godzilla realized it was
only a monster,
a figment of someone's imagination.

It cattle branded *ANXIETY*
on its chest and
tattooed *DEPRESSION*
across its forehead.

But I knew it was just a monster,
a fiction of my imagination:
my memories could be whole again:
I rebuilt my identity
with leftover pieces of the past,
sunshine, a sprinkling of optimism,
and two feet firmly planted
on higher ground.
I looked myself in the eyes
and found faith in humanity,
trust, and self-esteem.

Monsters never die.
They mellow with age.
Mine retired early,
bought a Cadillac,
and now lives in
a high-rise condo in Boca.

It still visits.
It still owns those tap shoes,
but I have learned
to tap-dance back.
I woke up one day,
got out of bed,
walked outside barefoot
to dewy grass
and rays of hope,
reached high in the air,
and took my smile back.

STARK RAVING

My madness convinced me
    to let it stay.
It told me it is
        the antidote
        to
        keep my
        pent-up anger
        at bay.
It claimed to be a beacon
            to
            shine a laser beam
            that
            will guide me through
            misguided, errant gaslighting,
It avowed that it could filter out
        all
        the yellow light
        so
        I can see colors
        as
        they actually appear.
It told me it will listen
      to all my concerns
            and
            keep accurate records
                  so
            I don't have to remember
                what
              I need to forget.

WHY I KEEP A MIDWIFE ON SPEED DIAL

Anger does not always happen as   screaming,
                                                    yelling,
                                        stomping of feet,
                                          fists clenching,
                                           teeth gritting,
                                         furrowed brows,
                                         tattered nerves.

Anger is not always   born of aggression.
It can be born   of hurt and confusion
                                 from a womb unaware
                  of the existence of its pregnancy
                                conceived via an act
                             of deception or betrayal
                              from a night of passion
                                  that materialized
                                into a morning after
                                  that transformed
                                   into an insidious,
                       compartmentalized ghost.

Anger is not always   loud.
Anger can exist   in silence and stagnation.
Anger may not have   hard edges
                                 that cut and bruise
                 all who come in contact with it.
It can be   soft.
It can be   amorphous,
made   of quicksand,

encompassing   its host

                               in suspended animation

causing   phantom paralysis

till   whoever owns it

realizes   the phantom

                               is a phantom,

                               a figment

                             of an emotion

                             or a feeling

                           or a reaction

             to a life event (or events)

                       that happened

                           in the past

that is exactly   what it is: the past

                       which can't exist

               in the present or future

                       due to the fact

                       that the past

                       can only exist

                          in the past

then the anger

starts to   shed its skin

to reveal   a hollow inside

that is   a breath long held

now   exhaled

               and

               let

               go.

YOUR SMILE NEVER CEASES TO EXIST AS
PART OF WHO YOU ARE

Remember
way back when your smile was your calling card?
when you smiled for more than happy?
when you smiled when were embarrassed?
when you smiled through a lie?
when you liked to smile?
when you used your teeth for more than chewing?

Remember
when you were always on?
then, you wanted to dim the lights a little.
attention felt like unattainable high expectations.
then, you reverted back to wallflower.
you were on vacation when you were present,
and no one knew but you.
silence was a place of comfort.

then, you crossed a threshold
when people started ending sentences
in conversations with you with question marks
that would not have had question marks in writing.

then, you stopped going barefoot around family
due to the myriad broken eggshells
they left on the ground
because it became mandatory
to walk on eggshells around you.

you felt hobbled by the unwritten rule
that everyone else was allowed to
stand up for themselves
but you must sit in the corner
like Dennis the Menace
as punishment for breathing.

but when you breathed you existed.
sometimes, the act of existence
is a form of standing up for yourself
even if you are unaware.

unwritten rules are unwritten
and thusly incapable of being set in stone.

the only things that
are truly set in stone
is that every human is composed
of blood, skin, and bones,
and every single person
decides how to use their teeth.

SURE YOU CAN AFFORD THE GAS BILL, BUT
THINK OF THE ENERGY YOU'LL SAVE

There are times when it's
best to stay quiet
and say nothing.

When you exercise
your well-honed
expertise in gaslighting,
it's often when
I refuse to react to
an obvious goat-getting comment.
When you change a subject
out of the blue
that has no relevance
to a conversation
and has the sole purpose
of button-pushing,
I have to weigh
whether to tell you
that my buttons
are on my clothes
and my belly button
is attached to my belly.

Don't announce
to the rest of the world
that I need to calm down
or not get excited
because I refuse

to acknowledge
the baseball bat
you have fashioned
into your tongue.

There is no human mouth
that wouldn't bleed
if a baseball bat
were inserted into it,
yet you do it to yourself
when you connect propane tanks
to your words and actions
to light up the sky that
is any conversation
you are part of
converting it
to a spectator sport
of which you are
the only competitor.

When I attend a baseball game,
I prefer to watch
without distraction.
Maybe squirt mustard
onto a soft pretzel
delivered by a teenager
carrying a Styrofoam ice chest
because it's okay
to just watch sometimes.
Try it, you might like it.

THE CARDIAC SURGEON WHO LIVES INSIDE
MY PSYCHE

I wish I could remove my heart
into a satin-lined box
every-now-and-then.

On the hottest summer nights,
when it's too hot for a top-sheet,
when i have several fans
strategically pointed at my bed,
when I exist in a constant hot flash.
On those nights,
if I dare fall asleep,
my dreams become a certain breed of warped.
On those nights,
the back of my neck sweats on to my pillow
till I wake to flip the pillow.

I sometimes wish I could remove my heart
before certain family events,
so my brain can lead my reactions
to the barrage of gaslighting I will endure
and strategically sew my mouth shut
for the sake of not making waves.
I should never stand up for myself
lest I be accused of shooting
a semi-automatic military gun
when I open my mouth.

If I could remove my heart
every time I run into someone

who had targeted me
for abuse in my past,
I would place it on a plate,
surgically slice a keloid scar
from its edge, place it
into a baby blue
Tiffany and Company
engagement ring box,
stand atop a chair,
and declare to the recipient:
You gave this to me
as if my future
was wedded to your
painfully obvious insensitivity
and need to control.
But you can't regift it,
because such scars' owners
must have a whole undamaged heart
that has never known
your warped vision of love.

Apologies to Mariah Carey.

WHEN THE CIRCADIAN BECAME RHYTHMLESS

You accused me of liking insomnia.
You said my insomnia wasn't real.
You said I only want to stay up late and watch tv.

You have had the privilege of never experiencing insomnia.
The word insomnia itself sounds like
everything it encompasses.

It is insidious.
It is laced with anxiety.
It is mentally painful
and physically painful
and mentally painful
and physically painful.

It is not a state of awake.

It is a trance trying to break free
from a place
it doesn't know
it exists in.

It is all the tears
that have escaped over the years
trying to find their way back to
the labyrinth of depression.

BECAUSE DERVISHES STILL WHIRL ON
HOTTER THAN JULY NIGHTS

I am standing still, stagnating
while the world around me
is swirling and twirling.
My existence is being dizzied
by whirling dervishes
that may only exist
in my imagination
by virtue of anxiety
or doctor-prescribed medication.

I feel I've fallen
into an eddy,
drowning,
trying to climb out,
fingers haplessly gripping
water droplets
to no avail.

But I am not in
any body of water
except maybe
a sweat-soaked pillow
on an extremely
hot, humid, unairconditioned
July night.

I stand by my assessment
that Stevie Wonder's
Hotter Than July

is undisputedly
one of the top 5
soul music albums of all time.

I'm no longer 54 but 14
obsessed with Stevie's music.
Having tried tequila for the first time,
having had one or two shots too many,
my brother Paul walks me
up two flights of stairs to my bedroom,
pushes his drunken brother
on to my bed
and walks away cackling
like a Shakespearean witch.
I'm on my back horizontally
on a vertically oriented bed;
my brain tries to instruct me
how to reorient my head to my pillow.
The ceiling starts spinning relentlessly
like a possessed Wheel of Fortune
minus a smiling Vanna White.

But this is just a memory
of a middle-aged man
living in self-imposed isolation
in a pandemic
who feels like
tiny tornadoes follow him around
selectively sucking
any common sense or creativity
left in his being

out from his brain
through his ear sockets
without lifting his substandard mass
into the airborne eddies.

Maybe I should follow
the advice of the mystic poets
who advise to celebrate life
by dancing instead of
watching others dance:
become a whirling dervish
in my own right
because the dervishes teach us
if we teach ourselves to whirl and twirl,
we are not culturally appropriating,
but we have learned
by watching them
how to not let life
make us feel falsely dizzy.

WHEN A HOUSEGUEST UNINTENTIONALLY
OVERSTAYS THEIR WELCOME

My dearest Isolation:
I will not cave in
to misguided emotions
and call this poem a love letter.
You have become my unlikely muse
in these days of wine and COVID.

What should I say?
You usually arrive in my life
during a depressive episode
or as a side effect of anxiety.
This time,
I chose to ask
for your company of loneliness
lo these many months.

At first,
you were a necessary roughness
then morphed into a secret lover,
cuddling close to me
under the down-alternative comforter.
I would feel sad
and you held my hand
which mysteriously morphed
into a hug.
Sometimes,
when you held my hand,
you'd raise it high in the air

and we'd find ourselves
atop a steep rollercoaster hill
that led into an endless loopty loop.

Every day,
I would open my laptop
and explore a world of poetry.
I stepped on stages
in New York, San Francisco, Nashville,
Paris, England, Ireland, Singapore,
and even way down in Old El Paso.
If Zoom gave airline frequent flyer miles
for after the pandemic,
oh the places I could go.

When restaurants closed,
the countertop kitchen appliances
climbed out of their cabinets.
I opened a James Beard Award-winning
residential single-client catering café
and wrote a best-selling poetry recipe book
that garnered me a tv show
on a cable channel that doesn't exist.

Isolation,
when I invited you to stay,
I found a muse.
I guess
I wasn't
as alone
as I thought I was.

THEY CALL ME HURRICANE BRAIN

All my nerves are last nerves.
Finality exists
as faulty serotonin snipers
missing targets
trying to hit bull's eyes.
They attempt to cross the bridge,
but the bridge was cut open
by a category 5 hurricane,
now sitting broken in Mobile Bay
with a 1/8-mile gap:
concrete, asphalt, and rebar
at the bottom of the bay
where crabs used to crawl.
The engineers must decide
whether it is feasible to
repair rather than replace,
but according to the science
of bridge architecture,
once a bridge breaks,
no band aids or plaster casts
can put Humpty Dumpty
back together again.
Pills are but a tool
in an intricate toolbox
serving as band aids for broken bridges
where serotonin tries
to connects us to happiness
but can't always curtail
the most common disease in the world
which consists of last nerves with finality.

BRIDGE-BURNER'S LAMENT

Is it possible to burn a bridge without lighting a fire?
Without accelerant to spread the flames?
Is it possible to burn more than one bridge at a time,
bridges that live miles away from each other?
Can bridges be so easily burned to a crisp with
one bad decision?
Can one bad decision cause
time-consuming daily detours
that cease being detours transforming
into permanent extended commutes?
The new age arsonist burns down
necessary structures with words and attitudes.
And unfortunately, ashes cannot
be used to resurrect the past.
Ashes composed of carbon black
will linger in the air and likely lead
to asthma and lung damage.
Of course, the arsonist never intended to burn bridges.
Of course, the river will still exist,
new bridges will get built,
and people crossing those bridges
when they come to them
will cross them as if
they were always there,
but their breathing will be plagued
with asthmatic wheezes
and constant coughs through lungs
scarred by someone else's bad decision.

FORGIVEN

I want to write a poem about forgiveness,
but
I am not sure
it will qualify
as a poem.
Maybe it will
just
be a list of regrets
of how I have chosen
to live my life.
I am unsure if
I am capable of forgiveness.
I am unsure if
I understand what this word is.
Besides
powerful and confusing.
Is forgiveness
an idea,
a construct,
an act of contrition?
When
I forgive someone else,
do I also
need
to forgive myself
for finding myself
in a situation
that might have been
beyond
my control?

Must I feel guilty
for
not giving closure
to someone
who has wronged me?
Am I allowed
to
forgive and not forget?
Or will that
just
be lip service
to a word
that is so arbitrary
in its parameters
it needs
to be seen
as
an idea or construct?
Is forgiveness an all or nothing deal?
Is total forgiveness achievable?
Can there be levels of forgiveness?
Does it exist on a spectrum?
Does it exist on a spectrum?
Does it exist on a spectrum?

Forgiveness:
you exist in my vocabulary,
but I have yet to define you.
I shall try to write a poem about you
so you can exist in totality.

HOW TO TURN YOUR HOME INTO AN INDOOR AMUSEMENT PARK

When dizzy happens,

                    you might sit or lie down
          to stop the room from spinning,
but when life continues

                    to spin out of control,
          everything that seems to
be on a forward trajectory

                    can act as a door stop
          for everything else.

Your overwhelmness

                    becomes a tumor
          hidden beneath your skin
no one knows about

                    unless they touch you,
          but you've successfully blocked touch
by allowing unlimited Reiki

                    while denying fingertip access
          with a level of deftness that
has them avowing   how smooth your skin is.

The fog released from

                    the breath of your words
          is a barrier that blocks
their sense of touch

                    from knowing it
          has not achieved touching.

You can be

                        as disoriented as possible
          while tricking the world your life is
an Olympic perfect-10

                      balance beam routine,
           because the gymnast on the beam
is a hired ringer

                        with your face
           temporarily tattooed to theirs.

Every room in your house is

                    a different dizzying ride:
           playground roundabout,
                    spinning teacups,
tilt-a-whirl,

              g-force astronaut training exercise.

You think if you practice enough

                   you'll become dizzy-tolerant,
but when you're punch-drunk-dizzy

                 more often than not,
          your tolerance will only
be visible in the fun-house-mirror

              you use while shaving away
          yesterday's bad decisions

                 every new today
in which you find yourself existing.

SO YOU'VE BEEN BANNED FROM EVERY
BOWLING ALLEY IN THE WORLD

Your laser-sharp tongue
that has cut so many people
from your life
can precisely skin and fillet
any fish in existence.
All types of bones
from all types of meats
are fare game
when you open your mouth
and wield
that hand-forged, Japanese-steel
Samurai sword of communication.

The bowling balls
your eyeballs transform into
when you roll your eyes
at anyone who disagrees with you
are perfect ammunition
for your conversational catapult
of insults and know-it-all-ism.

After two gold medals in biathlon,
you retired your rifle and crossbow
for a less conventional arsenal
to defend your compulsive-obsessive
social network of a life
from real connection.

All your admirers
are impressed with
your acumen for accuracy
with weaponry,
but those skills
make your friends
a bit reticent to invite you
to Thanksgiving, Sunday supper,
or even to care for their pet
when they leave for a weekend.

One day, you will die.
Those who knew you well
will decide how
you are remembered.
Your ability
to stir up a hornet's nest
where no hornet's nest ever existed
defines what happens
when you show up,
unsheathe your sword,
open your mouth,
causing everyone else
to bleed anxiety.

When you wield your words and actions
as an elaborate imaginary armory
rather than courtesy and kindness,
what others understand about you
will not be what you
want to be remembered for.

PROPER IRRIGATION TECHNIQUES FOR
HIGHWIRE TREES

There have been times
I have continued to cry
after my tear ducts ran dry.

Almond and avocado farmers
hire water well drillers
that use deep sea oil exploration drills
to tap previously untapped aquifers.
The earth's water
is not an infinite resource.
Farmers dig deeper and deeper every year,
yet I still continue to cry
when my tear ducts run dry.

Unlike the earth,
I will never run out of emotions.
I won't deny myself a good cry
which is my equivalent
of a balancing bar
for an unrepentant
highwire act life.

I understand
that my personal aquifers
are a limited resource.
I understand
I can't keep drilling
till I hit nothing

or maybe cry a little magma,
but crying on the inside
is an option that
has never worked out,
and I can choose
to let the highwire exist
without attempting
to ever cross it again.

THE AFTERLIFE OF A TEAR

Every tear I cry
tears a hole in my brain
to reserve a place
for a memory to reside.
Sometimes,
certain memories decide to burrow
a little further than the others
so when they get remembered
they have to be triggered.
Sometimes,
someone will commit a crime against me
I forgot I had previously experienced,
and I see the previous perpetrator's face
in the current perpetrator's face
which might make me scream loud enough
to make them go deaf.
There are memories
we want to remember forever.
There are memories
not consequential enough
to keep forever.
Then there are memories
that hide away in their burrowed holes
that leave permanent residue
in our souls called trauma.

BECAUSE YOU HAVE NOTHING TO BE
JEALOUS ABOUT

Allow me to introduce myself.
They say my skin is green,
But I ain't no Kermit the Frog.
I am Miss Piggy incarnate!
Honestly, my skin has no color,
not even black or white.

I will be your best friend if you let me.

Of course, you will:
because the enticing aroma of my pheromones
is akin to carbon monoxide
except there ain't no little box
you can put in your basement
or wire to your heart or soul to detect me.

When we show up at a social event,
I promise to make you
the life of the party.
If we don't get invited back,
It is their loss.

We got each other's backs and all that.
Our shit don't stink.
Our farts are made of carbon monoxide.
My toxicity has never killed anyone.

The more of me you breathe,
the more I will be your persona.

WE ARE ALL BORN PUGILISTS

We fight and we fight.
We punch and we punch.
Sometimes, we think
we have wrapped our hands
and put on gloves.
to look down
to bear witness
to bare knuckles.
Sometimes, there is no punching bag in front of us.
There is just air.
There is nothing in front of us
for our fists to connect with,
yet the empty before us
feels like punching a brick wall.

We exit our mother's wombs kicking and screaming
We are born fighting to enter this world.
Some of us continue to fight the rest of our lives.
We don't understand why we must always fight.
Sometimes, we don't realize
we are fighting
when we think
we are just breathing and surviving.

We allow bullies, bosses, abusive lovers.
to narrate our truths
with psychological and chemical warfare.
They speak the language of mustard gas
with words that burn through our self-esteem.

For some of us,
the act of waking up includes
installing brass knuckles
into our vocal chords
so our words become
weapons of mass protection.

For some of us,
our silence is self-flagellation
for allowing others
to guide the pens
with which we write our lives.
So we must relearn
to wrap our hands
and again wear the gloves
we were born wearing
when we kicked and screamed
our way into this world
so we do not have to write our futures
with our gloves on.

WHAT'S IN THE REARVIEW BELONGS
IN THE PAST

Do you live life
as if you are driving
in an infinite traffic jam
surrounded by ghosts?
As if you are a Ford Pinto
that will explode if hit from behind?
And your past is a garbage truck
manned by a drunk driver?

You look in the rear view.
History is aggressively tailgating you
honking loudly.
You switch lanes to let it pass,
but it decides to hang to your left
to flip you off.
The odors of every lesson you've learned
and every mistake you've made
wafts their way into your psyche.

You are aware this
is a ghost garbage truck.
You pull forward,
switch lanes directly in front of it,
and stop short.
Its ghostly phantasma passes through your Pinto
and dissipates into another universe.

Your psyche decides you are no longer a Pinto,
but a crosstown local bus
that may not always be on time
but gets you where you need to go
and a few places you never expected.

THE LEAST SWEET FRUIT ON PLANET EARTH

I am a connoisseur of sour grapes.
There are people who claim
to love the taste of sour grapes.
To be palatable,
sour grapes must always be
sweetened and/or spiced up exponentially.
Making sour grape jelly takes
an inordinate amount of sugar.
To ferment sour grapes,
one must submerge them in
at least 1 ½ times the volume of raw honey
for at least a month.
Sour grapes are most often used for vinegar,
but the vinegar can only
be used in small amounts.
No matter how sour grapes are consumed,
no matter how sour grapes taste
in their altered state,
sour grapes are
still sour grapes.
Sour grapes will always cause heartburn
in one way or another.

THEM WHO CONSPIRE
AGAINST PEOPLE WITH FEET

I believe
there is a conspiracy
afoot
between the manufacturers of shoes
and the makers of shoelaces.

Every time
I buy new shoes,
I tie them;
there always seems to be
at least a foot of shoelace
left on each shoe.
I double knot them,
yet
there is still enough shoelace
left over
that it is inevitable
that I will step on them.
Anyone who has stepped
on a double knotted shoelace
knows that
the bow gets pulled out
leaving an extremely tight knot
that can only be unknotted
by using a tiny screwdriver
or the tine of a fork
to unpretzel
the impossible pretzel.

New shoelaces
can cost
upwards of three or four bucks.
What a profit margin!
Enough, I believe
for certain unnamed shoe manufacturers
to get their kickbacks

THE PATRON SAINT OF DAMAGED GOODS AND EXCESSIVE BAGGAGE or IF I WERE A SAINT, WHAT COLOR WAX WOULD I BE?

During the first great nervous breakdown,

I purchased several prayer candles

from a Jamaican-run store in Queens.

          The tiny store front consisted

        of shelf after shelf of highball glasses

          with intricate drawings of saints

        filled with just about every color of wax.

It was like walking into a rainbow.

          A Rastawoman explained how

        each candle could enhance my existence.

A dozen patron saints filled my tiny abode

with the aroma of paraffin

and seduced me asleep

with fumes of futility.

          Should I wake and knock one over,

           I would burn down the existence

            of another tenement.

And after the wax was gone,

I had acquired one funky set of glassware.

THE PUPPYDOG THAT ATE A
BULLETPROOF VEST

My chest hair is made of sawteeth.
One day I woke, and the sheets were shredded.
Since my bed was a futon, cotton batting
was batting around the room.
There is no cure for this condition.
I always wear a Kevlar vest in case I have to hug someone.
After my heart was broken one time too many,
my body created a defense system
that blocks everything that approaches my heart.
Those sawteeth can't pick and choose what to shred.
When the saw was manufactured,
high-carbon Japanese steel was melted and mixed
with microscopic shards of diamond
then smelted and molded into a device, a tool
that never needs sharpening and is dishwasher safe
which is the safest way to rinse away emotional residue.
Too much emotion might make me cry
which can make life a little rusty,
and unfortunately, I'm allergic to WD-40.
I know I wasn't born when Murphy wrote his law,
but maybe Murphy's Law is a reason to
believe in reincarnation.
Maybe I think too much.
Maybe I think with my heart more than I should.
Maybe I should leave thinking to some other schmuck
who doesn't know better.
Unfortunately, it's too late to teach
this puppydog a new trick.
My condition and disposition are incurable.

WHEN YOU DON'T KNOW ALL YOUR WORDS
ARE TATOOED ON YOUR FACE

You told me my house was made of straw
and you were the big bad wolf.
Your words were hurricane-force winds
that blew my housed down.
I grew my next crop of hay in red clay
so my next home could resist you.

Then your words were made of fire
and my charred skin chipped away
revealing a leathery elephant hide
that was heat and flame proof.

So you ordered your words
to spit acid in my face.
but the tears that rolled over
the hardened scars on my cheeks
learned to repel you.

All your words,
even when you try to be nice,
are laced with ruinous disdain,
but when you speak at others,
you are actually talking to yourself.

Wind has permanently mussed
your stylish coif,
leaving you unkempt-looking.
Fire has singed your eyebrows,
permeating your warped conscience

with the putrid aroma
of burnt human hair.
All that acid you consumed
has etched nooks and crannies
into your soul
that can only be filled with regret.

Welcome to the mirror
you have chosen to live in.

LAND OF THE GLASS CATTAILS

For it has been told, a drunken angel fell to earth and
landed in a muddy marsh filled with cattails.
The marsh transformed: mud turned to silky sugar white
sand; cattails turned to glass.
There was no more darkness or rain.
Light refracted through the cattails producing little pieces
of broken rainbows that could cure a lost soul of life's ills.

Before you broke the glass cattails, you googled how to
snap a human soul in half like a twig.
You were wearing boots made for tromping through
marshes and snapping cattails like twigs.

When you broke the glass cattails, you made a decision to
break me as if I was crisp autumn leaves beneath your feet.
You had decided you were a giant and I was Jack come to
pillage your castle.

The day after you broke the glass cattails, you woke
wearing those boots.
They were fused to your feet, words, actions, and attitude.

When you left the castle, you and your boots bought an axe
to chop down a beanstalk: you needed to destroy my world
and bring me down to your level, but I live in a different
world where beanstalks grow beans and castles in the sky
are fiction.
I landed on my own two feet and walked away with more
than a few bumps, bruises, and scars.

I learned abusers are hunters and abused people often happen to be in the wrong place at the wrong time when a hunter is out sniffing for new prey.

What you never learned was that a person can't break someone else's soul, only their own.

As long as you choose to wear those boots, you'll be breaking off bits and pieces of your soul every day for the rest of your life.

In the place where the glass cattails grow, lost souls can only enter naked: no clothes, no boots.

Where the glass cattails grow, there is only sunlight, sand, glass cattails, and little pieces of broken rainbows that can cure a lost soul of life's ills.

BLEEDING

When I get cut, my blood flows from my skin
like lava from Kilauea.
Sometimes,
I need more than direct pressure to make it stay inside.
Sometimes,
I bleed recollections my subconscious
decides it's time to say goodbye to,
ones it held onto forming grudges
on the inside walls of my personality
that have aged enough to naturally
decay and chip away into history.
Sometimes,
I bleed bits and pieces of my childhood
I have hoarded away to create
an inflatable stunt mattress to break the fall
of obstacles and traumas of adulthood.
Sometimes,
my blood runs clear
forming inconsolable tears
when words are not available
to wrap my soul in warmth
when I've slipped and fallen
into consequential hypothermia.
Sometimes,
my blood is made of words
that form into poetry
when my tears and thoughts
pool together into poetry.
When that happens,
my blood no longer belongs to me.

WHEN HATE CRASHES A DINNER PARTY

In my youth,
thoughts stirring through
      my consciousness
        would sometimes
           jump
           into the outside world
   due to internal pressures
       causing a collateral
           exodus of spirit
             from my being
             whenever
          hate tried
          to enter
       without permission
         and grab my throat
           to choke out
          any common sensibility.
            But I didn't find
       such violence tempting
           and when hate
        grabbed my throat,
           I went limp
           and played dead
             till hate ran off
        before the police could arrive
        to find hate
           had murdered another soul
      despite that I was alive and well
   as could be with hate's
handprints fading from my neck.

WRONG TIME / WRONG PLACE

I walked only six or seven Manhattan blocks that afternoon,
yet in that short amount of time,
I completed my first marathon.
Colors no longer existed.
The world was gray like a black-and-white T V.
Everyone and everything around me was in slow motion.
Then I realized it was I that was in slow motion.
If you play a 45-rpm record on 78,
voices will sound like Chip and Dale
or Alvin and the Chipmunks.
If you play a 45-rpm record on 33 1/3,
voices will stretch into
an unintelligible,
perpetual piece of taffy.
Emotion no longer existed.
Exhalation no longer existed.
My lungs filled with bus and taxicab exhaust.
My every breath was asthmatic,
and I couldn't find any oxygen
for this new emblematic emphysema.
All the sudden, I was an ant
who accidentally returned to
the wrong mound of dirt,
and when I delivered a
microscopic piece of human-discarded
chocolate chip cookie crumb
to my queen, I realized this was not my queen
and this was not the first time in my life
I had arrived at the wrong place.

now you see me, now you don't

i am invisible.
i do not cross streets at crosswalks
or when traffic stops.
cars drive straight through me.

i am invisible.
at NASCAR races,
i do *The Hustle* in the middle lane.
the drivers do not see me:
they hit me head on,
yet i cause no accidents and never get injured.

i am invisible.
no one sees me.
i refuse to wear clothes when i attend weddings.
why not? no one sees me.

being invisible is hard work.
my boss often accuses me of goofing off
because he can't see me.
one day, i will proudly walk naked into his office
and piss in his desk drawer
where he keeps his fancy Mount Blanc pen
and gold-plated letter opener.
the security cameras won't see me enter or exit
or even see me pee because my pee is invisible,
but i do plan to eat lots of asparagus that day:
i am invisible, but i love causing a good stink
every now and then.

i am invisible.
when i cry, no one cares.
when i scream, people pretend to not hear.
when i laugh, i laugh alone.

the truth is i chose to be invisible.

sometimes, what seems like the easy way out,
turns out to be the most difficult path to take.

choosing to be invisible is
choosing to not be seen or heard.
choosing to be invisible is
choosing to be ignored.

when i chose to be invisible,
i no longer had to hide my emotions
and was able to remove my heart from my sleeve.

when i chose to be invisible,
i no longer had a shadow to be afraid of.

when i was young,
i was seen. i was heard.
when i laughed, others laughed.
when i cried,
they tried to wipe my tears.
when i screamed,
they covered their ears.
my shadow was a reliable companion.

when i looked in the mirror,
i saw myself, not someone i didn't want to be.
then, one day, i looked into a mirror
and saw someone i didn't want to see.
that day, i chose to be invisible
and exist to only me.

WHY WONDERBREAD IS THE TRUE EIGHTH
WONDER OF THIS WONDROUS WORLD

I am not Spiderman, but
I have climbed God-only-knows
how many walls in my lifetime,
my fingertips are so cut and calloused,
they barely have fingerprints,
but they are addicted to walls.
When I get to the top of a wall,
I turn into Humpty Dumpty,
and as I sit atop the wall,
the wall narrows and narrows
and I have a great fall,
but all the king's horses
and all the kings men
do not exist in my world,
and it never fails to be
one of those
so hot you could fry an egg days,
and when I hit the ground,
my shell breaks perfectly in half
and I turn into a perfect sunny-side-up egg.
The person who discovers me
calls the *Guinness Book of World Records*
who fly down in their corporate Concorde jet
then measure my diameter
and proclaim me to be
the largest sunny-side-up egg ever.
And since no one knows I was the egg,
the person who discovers me
gets a photo on the cover
of the New York Post
breaking my yellow
with a slice of burnt toast.

If I should ever climb a wall,
have a great fall,
and land sunny-side-up,
I hope whoever discovers me
calls *Ripley's Believe It or Not*:
they too have a corporate Concorde,
but they always travel with
at least a case of Wonderbread.
And Wonderbread makes
the most wonderful toast.

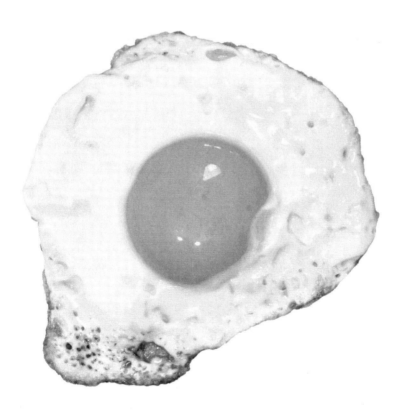

THE WAKE-UP CALL or WHY I LEFT
MY MATTRESS

I fell asleep
    and forgot to wake up.
I looked in the mirror
    and thought to myself
    This has to stop.
I lifted my head off a pillow
    that had formed quite a crater.
Although it was early morning,
    I had never woken later.

I breathed in through my nose
    and exhaled through my mouth.
A sigh that started the day I was born
    I finally let myself breathe out.

The sheets and spread
    were like layers of dead
    leaves on autumn ground.
I peeked at the sun
    through the blinds
    and the light made a
    magnificent sound.

I opened a window
    to let in a breeze
    and felt as if

I resided high in the trees.
I heard the birds of spring
        singing colorful songs I could see.
I fully opened my eyes
        and knew what had to be.

I walked barefoot,
        cool silky grass
        between my toes.
The aroma of pine and flowers
        created an other-worldly glow.
I let the sunshine in
        and inherited a whirling wind.
All the thoughts
        I refused to think
        were released by my psyche
        and exited through my skin.
My bed had been a suction cup
        coated with super glue.
But that day,
        I began to float.
        I even walked on air.
The day I finally woke up
        ended an endless nightmare
        and reminded me how to care.

CONFESSIONS OF A NECKTIE HOARDER or THE CLIP-ON CONSPIRACY

Awkward has always
been a word
that describes me.
Awkward conversations
might just be my specialty.
Appropriateness has no place
in my out of place reality,
manifesting a certain
lack of destiny,
a future undecided
because I'm indecisive;
to make a decision
would cause derision
in my shortsighted vision,
so visionary yet so stationary
compared to the speed of light,
the speed of sound and
the speed of other people's thoughts
having been thoughtfully thought out
so decisively and derisively
to point out my awkward ways
and the fact that
I always lose collar stays
that come with dress shirts
and I find ironing shirts
to be so therapeutic,
the sight of a crisp,
unwrinkled collar

that chooses not to choke me
makes me hesitant
to tie a tie tight enough to
make me feel relevant or
maybe even irrelevant
in the event
everything I think
is all in my mind.

Acknowledgements

I have been lucky to meet poets from around the world during the pandemic. It is important for me to acknowledge these people as both influences and friends.

Jane Spokenword, Rusty Rose, Martina McGowan, Henry L. Jones, and John McMullen are my new-found poetry heroes. The senses of humanity and self-awareness in their writing inspires me. I value the support, encouragement, and respect they have afforded me. I look up to them as role models and examples of the type of human being I want to be.

I can't say enough about my DaDa-Beat-Poet brother and fellow Beardo Bard of the Bardo Dane Ince whose talent and organization skills are amazing and whose friendship has been a source of support I find irreplaceable.

My loving sister, journeywoman and purveyor of elegant poetry Tricia *Phynne Belle* DeJesus-Gutierrez has been a consummate source of support and inspiration; our duet is a high point in my poetry journey.

Fellow Beardo Bard of the Bardo brother Mike Sindler has been a friend and taught me about structure, form, and trusting in my instincts and artistic decisions.

My Siamese twin and sweet soul goddess Marissa Prada has added so much goodness and happy to my life from the first time I heard her read poetry.

My friend LKN inspires me through his story and ability to translate drama into true emotion. He brings people from around the world together and creates safe spaces for creative expression. His poetry supersedes storytelling into otherworldly experiences.

The ever-positive Ron Marc Thomson and ball-of-energy Nick Paleologos are sources of encouragement, support, and friendship. Their poetry is like CPR for my soul when I feel down. This amazing poetry community has been given gifts-that-don't-stop-giving with their presence and dedication.

Special K, Catrice Greer, and Guy Biederman are valued friends and people I look up to for advice and as examples as successful, seasoned poets.

Open mic hosts Advocate of Wordz and LaBruja (Nuyorican), Christine Hall (Poetry in the Brew), Nazelah Jameson (Nomadic Press), Theresa Davis (Java Speaks), Richie Marufo (Barbed Wire), El David (Urban Beat Poet Society) David Leo Sirois Spoken World Online (or Paris)) have allowed me to be regulars at their events and created poetry communities that have weaved themselves into an international community. Also, Portland, Maine Poet Laureate Maya Williams who has revived Port Veritas into a truly welcoming event is my favorite breath-of-fresh-air host and a person I look up to as a poet and community leader.

Workshop facilitators Celena Diana Bumpus (who passed in February 2021), the mighty Peggy Robles Alvarado (Line Breaks and Bronx Beats), and workshop goddess Donna Snyder (Tumblewords) and Ralph Nazareth (Curley's) have taught me to trust my poetic instincts and pushed my writing to places I never knew it could go.

And Lady Poetry has helped to birth a version of myself that took me 55 years to look in a mirror and see a version of me I want to see.

Praise for *Everything Is All In My Mind*

Bryan Franco's first book, *Everything I Think is All in My Mind* highlights his abilities as a writer, wit, wry sense of humor, tongue in cheek observations of the world, and sensitivity to that same world. He sheds much-needed light on dealing with our monsters: human, emotional, and psychological while imploring us to stay the course of our personal labyrinthine journey and to take part in life's dance rather than sitting on the sidelines. He reminds us that we are never truly alone even in these tough times of isolation, which he has turned into one of his muses. He weaves clever and delicate details about himself, his personal struggles, and leaves breadcrumbs to help us find our way forward through humor and poetry.

- *Martina Green McGowan, MD, poet, author of I am the Rage*

Everything I Think Is All In My Mind makes you carve out time to enjoy – nay, devour it. Each word speaks to your psyche on an introspective level and makes you wonder how the author knows you as intimately as he does. This is one of those books you buy for a friend, then keep for yourself because you have dog eared your favorite poems and the spine is creased from repeated readings, so you have to buy a new copy to give to your friend.

- *Kimberly "Special K" Jay, poet, author of Journey to Forgiveness*

Everything I Think Is All In My Mind by Bryan Franco simply cannot be summarized in just a few words. Poets write poems to convey their deepest thoughts, emotions, and frustrations, packing every word, every line, every stanza with meanings that commune with the reader in a powerful way. This debut collection paints worldly images that come alive on the page. If you are looking for poetry to bring you to a space of shared human experience, you will dig this book.

- *Jane SpokenWord, jazz/beat poet, author of Word Against the Machine*

With penetrating insight and poetic agility, Bryan Franco's poems explore the wonders of wonder bread toast, clip-on tie conspiracies, and how the dances of the dervish may keep us from falling. Poignant and honest with generous helpings of humor and fantastic pace, *Everything I Think Is All In My Mind* is a provocative, well-crafted journey through the dark and the light, examining the costs of isolation, as well as the silver linings found through the portal of poetry and performance rendered with compassion, tears, smiles, and big-hearted love. This brilliant collection of poetry is everything you think it is. And more.

- *Guy Biederman, poet, educator, author of Nova Nights*

Everything I Think Is All In My Mind both engages and rages in a stream of consciousness giving us an outsider's view of the world. Health issues ranging from depression to obesity are written about with candid honesty and a little humour. Bryan Franco's debut collection has lines (and whole poems) herein, which need to be read and re-read.

- *Des Mannay, award-winning Welsh poet, author of Sod 'em – and tomorrow*

From the haikus at the beginning to the last words of *Confessions of A Necktie Hoarder*, no words are wasted in this debut collection. Bryan Franco not only writes poems that touch the very depth of feelings, he does it with, perhaps, some of the most amazing and inventive titles that lure you with the promise of something different. And once you're in, you are forever caught.

- *Fin Hall, Scottish poet, film maker, author of Once Upon a Time There Was, Now There Isn't*

Reaching the end of Bryan Franco's poetry collection feels like a death-defying fairground ride, vertiginous and all-shook up, but ultimately exhilarated and grateful for the experience.

- *Michael Durack, Irish Poet, educator, author of Flip Sides*

Everything I Think Is All in My Mind is a guide for what depression and anxiety looks like from within. Bryan Franco's poetry relays a message that answers aren't always readily available, and we are all works in progress. His writing is unapologetic, honest, charismatic, genuine, and comical.

- *John Chance Acevedo, poet, educator, host/curator, author of Blame It on April*

From beginning to end, *Everything I Think Is All In My Mind* is a whirlwind of discovery, humor, and honesty. Bryan Franco's poetry is both silly and sincere and resonates. His use of isolation as a time of community building reminds us of the joys of being alive along with the importance of words amidst the struggles of mental health and other unplanned sorrows and questions.

- *Maya Williams, poet, host of Port Veritas, Portland Maine Poet Laureate*

Everything I Think Is All In My Mind presents a mouthwatering recipe for Bryan Franco's poetry, the main ingredient being the ability to observe one's own life experience patiently and keenly. He marinates his words thoroughly in near virtuoso insight and generously seasons them with sometimes irreverent, but always on point wit. This book will never leave you wanting for food for thought; you'll be satiated and ready to line up at the lexicon buffet for seconds.

- *Tricia DeJesus-Gutierrez, poet, host of*
Phynnecabulary and The Poet's Lighthouse, author of
Some Days Here

Bryan Franco's wit, gentle humanism, and joie de vivre are all evidenced in this collection of close observations and sensual ruminations. In *Everything I Think Is All In My Mind,* he skillfully slides through styles ranging from formal haiku to fluid prose poems and monologues displaying his signature tragicomic voice. You need not experience one of his beloved open mic performances to feel the sincerity and lyrical dexterity this unpretentious poet brings to the stage. You need to only open the volume in your hands and enjoy.

- *Michael Sindler, Poet, workshop facilitator, Beardo*
Bard of the Bardo

What a year it has been, and the poets who continue to create, in spite of, truly shine. Bryan Franco is one of these poets, whose collection *Everything I Think Is All In My Mind* reminds us that poetry can still heal; whether you are a champion emotional cyclist or just trying to avoid sink holes, this collection is for you. With fantastic titles that feel like poetic headlines, Bryan shares the news of his psyche and has sprinkled a bit of it on each page. So, be careful when opening this book, you might get some brain on you.

- *Thomas Fucolaro, poet, educator, cofounder of Great*
Weather for Media, author of It Starts from the Belly
and Blooms

About the Author

"Generalissimo" Bryan Franco hosts Café Generalissimo Open Mic and is a member of Beardo Bards of the Bardo with Dane Ince and Michael Sindler. He has been published in Love Letters to Gaia, Poetry in the Brew Sinew, 2020 Writing from Inlandia, Moonstone Arts Nonsense Verse, Moonstone Arts, The American War Against Itself, Moonstone Arts 25th Anniversary Poetry Ink, Globalization (Australia), Same Page (Ireland), and Puppycat anthologies; also, Anecdote, Down in the Dirt, and CC&D literary magazines.

He has featured for They Call Me Mitch, Mahopoc Writers, 1428 Poets, Word is Write, Glasgow Scotland Stay At Home Fringe Fest (with the Beardos), Creative Expressions NYC, Port Veritas, Why Open Pandora's Box, Eyepublishewe Poets Celebrate Our Dead, Time to Arrive, and Like a Blot From the Blue, (Scotland), Write & Release (England), Spoken World Online a.k.a. Paris (Canada) also, Phynnecabulary, Poets of the East, and Friday Night Live (Ireland) podcasts.

He has also facilitated workshops for Tumblewords Project and Phynnecabulary Poetry Games.

Facebook: generalissimo bryan franco
Instagram: @gnrlsmo
Email: francobryani@gmail.com
Linktree: https://linktr.ee/generalissimo
PayPal: _paypal.me/bryanirafranco